MAJOR BATTLES IN US HISTORY

# THE INVASION OF NORMANDY

## EPIC BATTLE OF WORLD WAR II

by Moira Rose Donohue

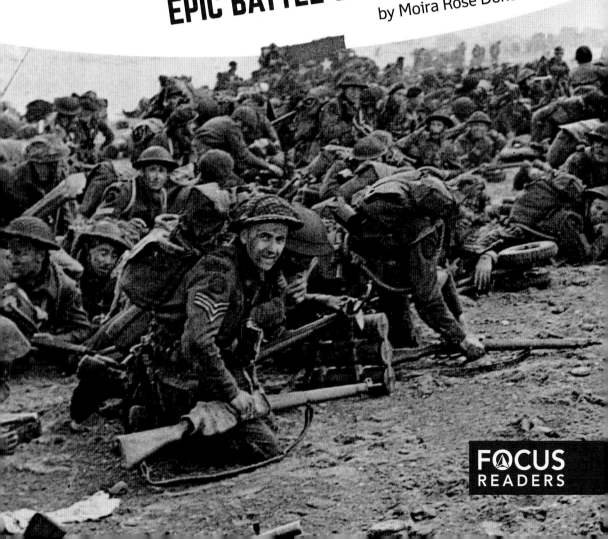

FOCUS READERS

# WWW.NORTHSTAREDITIONS.COM

Produced for North Star Editions by Red Line Editorial.

Photographs ©: AP Images, cover, 1, 23; Red Line Editorial, 5, 11; US Coast Guard/AP Images, 6–7; Library of Congress, 9; Everett Historical/Shutterstock Images, 12–13, 16–17; Keystone Pictures USA/ZumaPress/Newscom, 15; cornishman/iStockphoto, 19; DK Images, 21 (left); Dorling Kindersley/Thinkstock, 21 (right); US Maritime Commission/Library of Congress, 24–25; Everett Collection/Newscom, 27; Peter J. Carroll/AP Archives/AP Images, 28

Content Consultant: John J. Tierney, Jr., PhD, Walter Kohler Professor of International Relations, Institute of World Politics, Washington, DC

**ISBN**
978-1-63517-024-5 (hardcover)
978-1-63517-080-1 (paperback)
978-1-63517-184-6 (ebook pdf)
978-1-63517-134-1 (hosted ebook)

**Library of Congress Control Number: 2016951030**

Printed in the United States of America
Mankato, MN
November, 2016

# ABOUT THE AUTHOR

Moira Rose Donohue practiced law for 20 years before becoming a children's author. She has written more than 20 books for young people, both fiction and nonfiction. She loves dogs, hockey, and tap dancing. She and her husband divide their time between northern Virginia and Saint Petersburg, Florida.

# TABLE OF CONTENTS

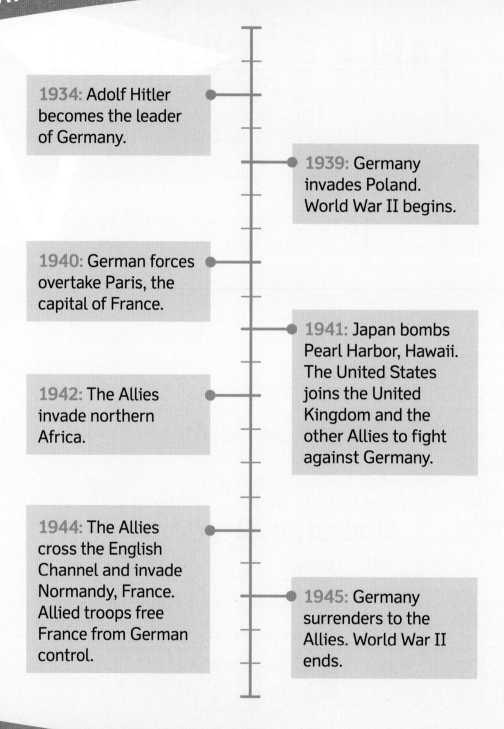

**1934:** Adolf Hitler becomes the leader of Germany.

**1939:** Germany invades Poland. World War II begins.

**1940:** German forces overtake Paris, the capital of France.

**1941:** Japan bombs Pearl Harbor, Hawaii. The United States joins the United Kingdom and the other Allies to fight against Germany.

**1942:** The Allies invade northern Africa.

**1944:** The Allies cross the English Channel and invade Normandy, France. Allied troops free France from German control.

**1945:** Germany surrenders to the Allies. World War II ends.

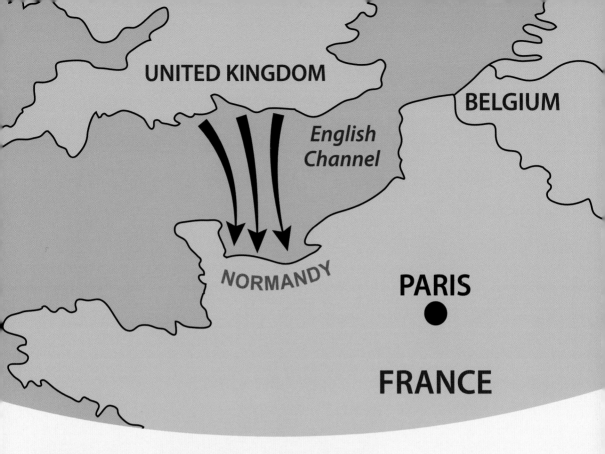

UNITED KINGDOM

BELGIUM

*English Channel*

NORMANDY

PARIS ●

FRANCE

## NORMANDY INVASION CASUALTIES

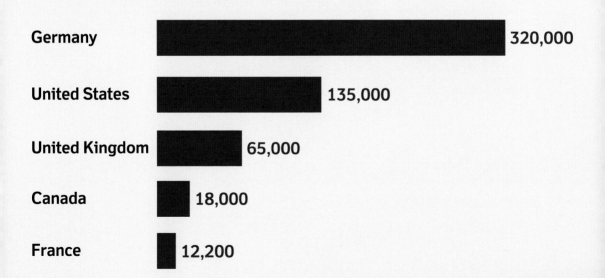

| | |
|---|---|
| Germany | 320,000 |
| United States | 135,000 |
| United Kingdom | 65,000 |
| Canada | 18,000 |
| France | 12,200 |

# CHAPTER 1

# D-DAY

The English Channel was choked with British and US warships. Darkness and fog cloaked them as they moved toward the shores of France. But as daylight sliced through on June 6, 1944, the soldiers in the small, flat-bottomed boats could see the beach ahead.

US troops take a transport boat to the beaches of Normandy, France, on June 6, 1944.

The watercraft, called Higgins boats, bobbed and rocked with the waves. Some men in the Higgins boats looked at photos of family and girlfriends. Others bowed their heads or touched prayer beads.

General Dwight D. Eisenhower, commander of the Allied forces, had told the troops, "We will accept nothing less than full victory!" They had to defeat the German army on the beaches of Normandy, France. It was the most effective way to **invade** western Europe.

Booms like thunder came from behind the Higgins boats. US warships fired at the concrete forts, called pillboxes, on

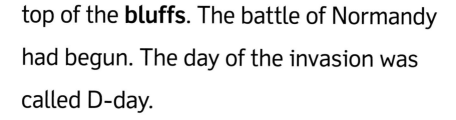

Dwight D. Eisenhower speaks to members of the US Army's 101st Airborne Division on June 5, 1944.

top of the **bluffs**. The battle of Normandy had begun. The day of the invasion was called D-day.

The Higgins boats sailed close to the shore. Their front panels dropped open. The panels became ramps. Soldiers trudged down the ramps into cold water up to their waists.

Enemy bullets pinged against the ramps and splashed into the water. The soldiers were shocked. They thought Allied planes and ships had destroyed the pillboxes. But German soldiers were firing machine guns from inside the small forts.

On the beach, crossed steel beams lined the sand. These structures were nicknamed hedgehogs. They were part of the Atlantic Wall the Germans had built to keep warships from landing on the beach.

Some soldiers raced onto the beach and took cover behind the hedgehogs. But many soldiers did not make it that far.

# THE ATLANTIC WALL

The Atlantic Wall did not stop the Normandy beach landing. But it forced the Allies to create vehicles that could both float on water and drive on land.

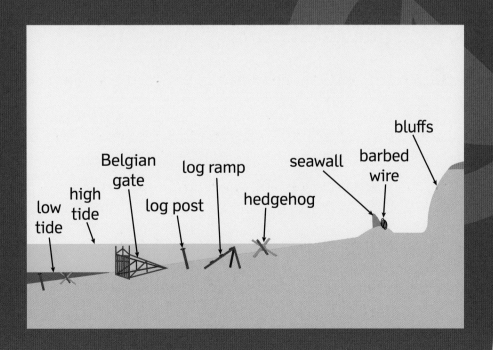

# CHAPTER 2

# PREPARING FOR WAR

In 1934, 10 years before the battle of Normandy, Adolf Hitler became the führer, or leader, of Germany. Hitler told the world he wanted more land for his country. But what he really wanted was to conquer as many countries as he could and to eliminate entire groups of people. Hitler sent his army to nearby countries.

**Hitler (standing) believed Germans were superior to people from other places.**

Hitler put these countries under German rule. Soon, a world war broke out. Hitler's troops killed millions of **innocent** people because of their race and religion. People around the world were outraged by Germany's actions.

The United States stayed out of the war at first. But on December 7, 1941, Japan attacked Pearl Harbor, Hawaii. Japan was Germany's ally. The United States joined the United Kingdom, Canada, and other countries to fight back. This group of countries was known as the Allies.

Hitler knew the Allies would try to enter Europe from the north. But he did not know when or where. The Allies

The Allies created fake tanks and airplanes to mislead the Germans about the location of the invasion.

tried to keep Germany unsure of where they would attack. They sent misleading messages and created distractions. The true time and location of the attack was kept secret, even from the Allied soldiers.

# CHAPTER 3

# OPERATION NEPTUNE

The Germans thought the Allies would attack in the spring. They expected the invasion to occur during the daytime and at high **tide**. But Eisenhower had other ideas. He wanted to start at night when there was only a half-moon. June 5, before sunrise, would be perfect. He decided that would be D-day.

**Allied soldiers load ships on June 1, 1944, in preparation for D-day.**

Bad storms hit early in June. The Allies needed clear skies to fly planes over the beaches before landing there. The rain and clouds were supposed to continue, so on June 4, Eisenhower delayed his plan. Late in the evening of June 5, Eisenhower got a new weather report. The clouds were breaking up. He also received a **decoded** message from the Germans. It indicated that Hitler knew about the buildup of troops in the southern United Kingdom. But Hitler thought it was a distraction. He would not send extra troops to Normandy. Eisenhower decided to go ahead with his plan, known as Operation Neptune, the next morning. Allied troops would land on five Normandy beaches on June 6.

While it was still dark, Allied planes bombed German pillboxes atop the bluffs overlooking the beaches of Normandy.

# THE BEACHES OF NORMANDY

Allied forces spread their attack over 50 miles (80 km) and five beaches. More than 5,000 ships and 13,000 aircraft were involved in the attack.

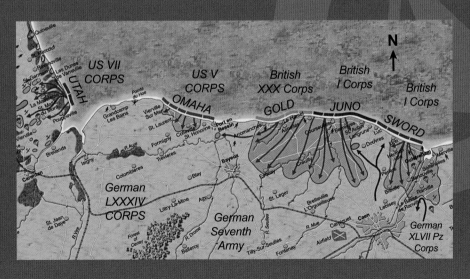

But the weather was windy and cloudy. The pilots missed many of their **targets**. The Allies also flew **paratroopers** behind the enemy to capture bridges and roads. But the wind shifted. Many men were pushed off course. Others were shot down by German soldiers.

As soon as it was light outside, the Higgins boats sailed up to the beaches. They carried soldiers, trucks, and tanks. The tanks, called Sherman DDs, were supposed to float to shore. But they were swallowed by rough waves. All but three sank. A strong tide pulled some of the landing craft off course. Despite the difficulties, soldiers scrambled up the steep beaches. They pitched dynamite into the pillboxes. They blew up barbed wire fences with **torpedoes** fired through long steel tubes called bangalores. Meanwhile, the German army was confused.

## THE TANKS OF D-DAY

Sherman DD

A waterproof screen could be raised and lowered. When raised, the screen allowed the tank to float.

Sherman Crab

Spinning chains cleared a path free of mines and barbed wire.

Some phone lines were down. And German generals received conflicting reports. Some heard paratroopers had landed near Calais, France. But this turned out to be a distraction. Finally, one German officer at Normandy got through to the generals over the phone. He held up the receiver so they could hear the gunshots.

It would take time for the German tanks and troops to get to Normandy. But a couple of German pilots were nearby. They jumped into their planes and flew to Normandy, where they shot at Allied soldiers on the beaches. German field marshal Erwin Rommel said that once

Allied troops at Utah Beach take shelter before moving inland.

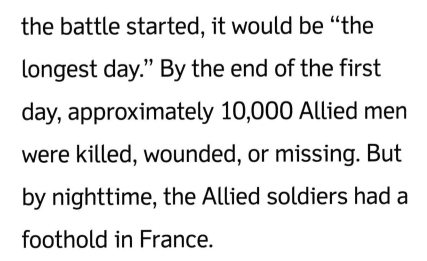

the battle started, it would be "the longest day." By the end of the first day, approximately 10,000 Allied men were killed, wounded, or missing. But by nighttime, the Allied soldiers had a foothold in France.

# CHAPTER 4

# OPERATION OVERLORD

The Allies took the beaches and moved inland. The invasion, called Operation Overlord, had begun. Now the Allied soldiers faced another problem. In the United Kingdom, many farms were separated by rows of low bushes called hedgerows. But in France, the hedgerows were tall mounds topped with trees.

**Allied forces unload onto Omaha Beach. The Allies used balloons to protect their troops against air attacks.**

Deep ditches lined either side of the hedgerows, and shrubs covered the sides. Soldiers got lost and confused because of the hedgerows. German soldiers hid in the ditches. As the Allied soldiers climbed over the hedgerows, they often came face-to-face with German rifles.

The British and Canadians fought their way south to Caen, France. The Americans pushed farther west and then turned around. The Allied armies planned to meet at Falaise, France. The fighting continued for two months. Finally, by mid-August, the Allies had almost surrounded the Germans at Falaise.

Overgrown hedgerows could easily conceal soldiers waiting to attack.

The Allies squeezed the German soldiers into an area with only one way out. This became known as the Falaise Pocket. The Allies kept up the pressure by bombing the German troops.

American soldiers march through Paris on
August 29, 1944.

On August 20, 1944, the Allies
surrounded the German army and closed
the gap. The Germans were beaten.
The battle of Normandy was over. On
August 25, Allied soldiers marched into

Paris, the capital of France. French people waved their nation's flag. The bells of Notre-Dame Cathedral rang. France was free from German rule.

Winning the battle of Normandy changed the course of World War II (1939–1945). It gave the Allies control in the north of Europe. It also started a losing streak for Germany, and on May 8, 1945, the German army surrendered.

Today, children chase waves and build sandcastles on the Normandy beaches. But on top of the bluffs are rows of graves and the remains of some pillboxes. They remind visitors of the lives lost during the battle of Normandy.

# FOCUS ON
# THE INVASION OF NORMANDY

*Write your answers on a separate piece of paper.*

**1.** Summarize the events in Chapter 2 that led to the United States entering World War II.

**2.** The Allies put a lot of effort into giving the Germans false information. Do you think this work paid off? Why or why not?

**3.** What was the name of the Allies' floating tank?

  **A.** Higgins
  **B.** Sherman DD
  **C.** Sherman Crab

**4.** What negative result might have occurred if Eisenhower delayed the invasion of Normandy?

  **A.** German leaders might have realized where the attack was coming from.
  **B.** The Allies might have been less prepared.
  **C.** The Allies might have had an easier time crossing the English Channel.

*Answer key on page 32.*

# GLOSSARY

**bluffs**
High, steep banks or cliffs.

**decoded**
To have found out something's true or hidden meaning.

**innocent**
Free from guilt, blameless.

**invade**
To enter in large numbers in order to conquer or take over.

**paratroopers**
Soldiers trained to jump with parachutes out of planes.

**targets**
Objects to be shot at.

**tide**
The constant change in sea level.

**torpedoes**
Self-propelled cylindrical weapons.

# TO LEARN MORE

## BOOKS

Demuth, Patricia Brennan. *What Was D-Day?* New York: Grosset & Dunlap, 2015.

Samuels, Charlie. *D-Day.* New York: Gareth Stevens, 2014.

Williams, Brian. *The Normandy Beaches.* London, UK: Arcturus, 2011.

## NOTE TO EDUCATORS

Visit **www.focusreaders.com** to find lesson plans, activities, links, and other resources related to this title.

# INDEX

**Answer Key: 1.** Answers will vary; **2.** Answers will vary; **3.** B; **4.** A